RANTS RAVES & WORDS OF WISDOM

by Jeffrey Laursiton

Dedication

I dedicate this book to myself (Rants), Cara (Raves) and to Jesus (Words of Wisdom)

Acknowledgment

First, I would like to thank Jesus for the creative skills which he has so kindly bestowed upon me. I would also like to thank Cara, for helping to inspire some of the writings as my muse. I also thank Facebook for being a medium of sorts in allowing me the opportunity to share my work with the world.

Introduction

This book is a collection of poems and rhymes which were initially published on Facebook, so I would be able to transfer my work in book form later. This is a collection of various works of mine published on social media only to help facilitate in getting my work copywritten much sooner. I'm certain that you will find my work to be tasteful with some added spice. Enjoy!

You're My Everything:

Give me thirty seconds
And I'll give you sixty reasons
Why love is the greatest weapon
Throughout all and any season

Give me one hour
And I'll show you twenty four ways
How love has the power
To help bring forth more brighter days

Give me one week
And I'll give you thirty kisses
On your lips your head and cheek
Then ask you to be my misses

Give me one month
And I'll give three hundred sixty five
...Ways that I won't
Ever stop from keeping hope alive

Give me that year
And I'll show you for a lifetime
How much I hold you dear
And how you are my lifeline

Give me thirty seconds
Because that's all I'll ever need
Since I've got God's blessing
Which enables us to proceed

Love You Cara

~Jeffrey Lauriston

My Best Friend:

I'm trusting you Lord
I'm trusting you God
Your word is my sword
And your precepts my rod

I'm counting on you Jah
You are all that I have
Praises and hallelujahs
Are sung to you with laughs

Lord God I call out to you
For it's you alone who knows
...All that I have been through
Though I hardly let it show

Father I am far from a saint
I have done many wrongs
When & where my heart's faint
You sustain & make me strong

Jesus you are my everything
Thank you for opening doors
It is with much joy that I sing
Hymns of praises from the core

Lord God you are that you are
For you have and always been
Whether you are near or far
You are still my best friend

~Jeffrey Lauriston

Family:

I got a chance to speak with my aunt this eve
All thanks are due to my awesome uncle Steve
Some things in life shouldn't be hard to believe
Like how vastly important family really is

Others may not be used to that concept
Having a strong family unit so to rep
By rep I mean being able to fully represent
Especially when it's evident fam is heaven sent

My late father Jean and my late gramps Stenio
Never ever ever would just let their family go
When it came down to such a hapless scenario
Those two right there sure did not play the radio

Then you've got my great uncle Mandvil
And his late brothers Marc and Man (Mon)
Those three also did not play the radio still
Not even a little bit especially not for fun

I got a chance to speak with my aunt Nadine
Would you believe that she's a beauty queen
I also got a chance to chat with my uncle Mo
Water may be sweet but blood is thicker though

~Jeffrey Lauriston

Stop The Bloodshed:

Father God I ask that you please save us
Look at what just happened in Vegas
Not that long ago it happened in Orlando
This has to be a movie but it's not Fandango

I almost forgot about the plot in Barcelona
When Abouyaaqoub plowed in on La Rambla
Why must there be such destruction and pain
Likened to what happened this year in Spain

We've got wars and terror running rampant
We do not want this world to be left in remnants
We have to open up our hearts and our minds
It seems like the blind are now leading the blind

These world and domestic conflicts are crucial
The lives being lost and bloodshed is brutal
I know as a people we can come to do better
We must help out one another to the letter

Father God my heart is crying out for Vegas
We're sending up petitions along with prayers
Please Father Jesus you must help to save us
We walk by faith as we give you much praises

~Jeffrey Lauriston

Dog Days:

You know that I want you in the worst way
The same way from the very first day
Indeed I did gladly give my heart away
That was by design so that I wouldn't stray

You grow more beautiful each day anew
I still have yet to meet another like you
I'm not looking since I already have you
I mean women like you are far & are few

You plus me I think that equals two
At the alter is where I wish to rendezvous
Thru sickness & health poverty & wealth
I promise I will always be there for you

You're amazing in everything that you do
It's not my fault that I'm amazing too
I could revert and go back to my old ways
It drove me berserk living in those dog days

It's a new time new day new dawn and such
Nothing has changed I do love you much
It's every minute your name rolls off my tongue
Cara my dearest you've got this brother sprung

~Jeffrey Lauriston

Solid Ground:

God you have searched my heart
You yourself know what I desire to do
Helping to motivate and inspire is an art
Which I have come to learn from you

Father we took a walk together not long ago
You prevented me from going to the desert
You showed me signs in which way I should go
I appreciate your kindness and your efforts

Jesus Lord I thank you for giving me a chance
To find a church where I was able to sing & dance
It seems like everyday you give me a great surprise
Only to make me stronger & stable in your eyes

I've learned to trust in you in not in my own ways
After all I've been through I'm glad to see more days
Your light shines upon me likened to the sun's rays
I will follow you blindly with much reverence & praise

Thank you thank you thank you is all that I can say
For sending something real in my life here to stay
You have taken all my worries & turned them around
I'm always feeling humbled as I walk on solid ground

God you alone knows what's in my heart
You forged and have written my path from the start
Jesus you have brought peace in my life once more
I'm now able to thrive you've help to make me secure

~Jeffrey Lauriston

My Cara-Line:

She is my one and only
Never prone to leave me lonely
At first she thought I was a phony
Until she came up right up on me

Convinced that my love is for real
We went ahead and sealed the deal
Now I'm loving how I feel
I'm living life with much more zeal

I've been through downs and ups
And ups and downs all of the time
There has been nothing but ups
Ever since I've met my Cara-Line

She does this very special something
And I mean she does it all of the time
Which is to give a strong love lasting
...It is in her love where I best shine

She's definitely my one and only
I promise I won't betray her trust
Our God above who has made her for me
Is there to protect the both of us

~Jeffrey Lauriston

My Girl:

I had such a great time on yesterday
Going this way and that way
There were some Goodfellas on display
Bringing our love back on instant replay

You are the greatest love I have even known
You make me happy by being who you are
I don't ever want to leave a love like yours alone
Which has been so sensational thus far

Cara you definitely are a different breed
It's almost like you've got the Midas touch
In you is found everything I'll ever need
I'm reaching out to let you know I love you much

You always find ways to crack me up
Forcing a smile when there's no reason to laugh
That's just your way of trying to lift me up
I kiss the Hands of Destiny that we crossed paths

I remember how sad I was last year
Before my angel descended upon my life
That is part of the reason why I hold you dear
I can't imagine another woman being my wife

I've had a great time these past few days
Your love was designed to simply amaze
I'm so glad that God has sent you my way
When it's cold outside I've got the month of May

~Jeffrey Lauriston

Christmas In Fall:

Cara dear I love you just like the sunrise
You're my Forever Lady you'll always be my baby
Never did I imagine that life would be this nice
You make a brother sane again no ifs or maybe

Cara my angel dove you're the greatest of all
Santa Clause gave to me Christmas in the fall
Every day is a celebration as I enjoy my gift
It's your loving sensation that helps to uplift

You are the greatest miracle I've ever seen
At times I can be cynical you're still MY Queen
What I'm trying to say is I trust you all the way
It's been a while since placing trust in a babe

Since you are my backbone I'm forever brave
Don't worry for you are the only one I crave
I'm glad you joined the line up so I can see
Just how much of a blessing God gave to me

Cara dear I love you just like the moon light
Everything was wrong and you made it all right
I should have written earlier but I was in pain
Until I met up with you to help me heal again

~Jeffrey Lauriston

My Redeemer Lives:

The graces of the Father are ever upon us
He cares for maintains and loves us
I'll be the first to shout out my hallelujahs
For this glorious life given by my Savior

We may stumble but we will not falter
Our endgame & destination is still the alter
I'm coming to thank you oh Heavenly Father
For endowing me with a unique sense of culture

Father God I will give you praises for all my days
You've done more for me than I could have asked
Show to me your precepts so to learn your ways
Every time you've called I've been up to the task

As we mentioned earlier on all things are possible
Once you have Christ in your hearts and minds
Succeeding while living a simple life is probable
With success do not forget to be humble and kind

The love of the Father above is ever upon us all
The Great Redeemer will keep you standing tall
While walking recently I saw a message on the wall
Which reminded me on who's name I should call

I Love You Jesus

~Jeffrey Lauriston

A Breath of Fresh Air:

You bring such a good vibration...
With you when you come around
I tell everyone in this great nation
...That you are the best in town

Every day is a celebration...
Getting a chance to kick it with you
I tell you true with no hesitation
That women like you are far and few

What a wonderful thing it is to know
That the power of the Most High ever flows
That the love of the Most High will not stop
I was way at the bottom He took me to the top

I'm beginning to learn how to let go & let God
Better able to discern what is normal or odd
I have God with me who lifts me off my feet
My God is a big G His love makes me complete

The vibe that you bring is like a breath of fresh air
Any time I call your name you are always there
Father Jesus thank you Lord for this new day
I'm confident that your love is really here to stay

~Jeffrey Lauriston

Mission Is Possible:

They said that the mission was impossible
That I would end up in the hospital
See with Christ everything is possible
He works in the Super and not the natural

I talk to Jesus like we are best friends
And we really are best friends till the end
The beauty of it all is that there is no end
This is the same Christ who died & rose again

We serve a grand and very mighty God
It doesn't matter if you're home or abroad
If you were to earnestly pray with all of your heart
He will give you another chance for a fresh start

I am simply amazed by His love and His grace
He consistently continues to bless this place
There are memories and views we can't erase
Still that is no excuse not to seek His face

Father God I thank you for all you've done
I am happy and content with my special someone
Cara dear I love you and please do no longer fear
I promise I won't leave & I'm truly being sincere

~Jeffrey Lauriston

Just Like An Angel:

Cara have I told you that I love you
And how much you mean to me
In you there is so much value
That only my naked eyes can see

You are lovely and I only desire...
To be with you for all of my days
You've helped to lift my spirit higher
By showing me you want me to stay

Now that my eyes are wide open
And see the loyalty and respect
You just keep my love for you growing
I guess your sweetness has that effect

I love you Cara like no other
You're the greatest woman I've ever loved
You helped to rescue me from the slaughter
Just like an angel from up above

Cara let me remind you how I love you
You've earned and have gained my trust
I will always find ways to be there for you
Only because loving you is a must

~Jeffrey Lauriston

Sweet Pea:

Cara Sweet Pea
I really appreciate what you bring
It once was you without me
Now both our hearts can sing

Maybe I'm sappy and over the top
That's to be expected...love don't stop
I know now that we can make it
Your tender heart I will not break it

Babe I've wrong you in the past
Please forgive me is all I ask
Not a day goes by without asking why
God decided to make me such a lucky guy

Sweet Pea your love is something terrible
Only because you are so incredible
You are also so very much edible
But we're not going to go there though

Cara Sweet Pea
You are very much appreciated
It is still so very amazing to me
How your love is more than I anticipated

I Love You Cara

~Jeffrey Lauriston

Beautiful Life:

What a wonderful and beautiful life
I'm this close to finally having a wife
I love this woman like nothing else
She's my number one indeed top shelf

Cara you're awesome beautiful and fine
You're the creme of the crop & top of the line
I love you more & more with each passing day
You're terrific in just about every which way

Cara oh me oh me oh my my
I must say that you've captured this guy
You've taken me to places I've never dreamed
I'm so very fortunate to have you on my team

Cara I love you like nothing ever loved
You're my angel my dearest you are a dove
Today I had a very fantabulous day
Who comes up with fantabulous I do but hey

What a wonderful and very vivid life
I'm really this close to having a wife
Everything is cool real calm and nice
If I ever loved you once I now love you twice

~Jeffrey Lauriston

Tree of Life:

How much more beautiful could it be
Having something sacred to keep
I understand now I can clearly see
Just skirted around a little me being me

Now that I am free and happy again
We can keep pressing forward towards a win
We are all winners under the sky
We just have to remember that...you & I

Here is the balance we sought for a while
Left is to right as up is to down
Alignment of higher principles are at play
Thank you Dear Jesus is all I can say

What a wonderful life this is to me
To have a great companion to help humble me
I'm feeling much better I guess love can heal
I wish everyone could feel how happy I feel

Jesus you've answered all my prayers
I love you I love you as I'm sure you're aware
I praise your Name you're the greatest of all
If ever I am leaning you help me to stand tall

I Love You Jesus

~Jeffrey Lauriston

Happy:

I love you young lady
Oh how I really do
There's no if buts or maybes
Just how much I'm feeling you

Last night you woke me up
While I was fast asleep
When you looked in my eye cups
I knew you were the one to keep

I will call you my number one
Know there is no number two
Cara I've loved you for so long
Your love helps make me fast & strong

You are so majestic in your ways
And have such a soulful gaze
Cara I see something in you
Which can only be seen by few

I love how you're so sweet
Admire how you keep me on my feet
You're the most beautiful in my eyes
You make me such a happy guy

I Love You Cara

~Jeffrey Lauriston

Mirror Mirror:

Hey babe I writing to let you know you're missed
You left yesterday without so much a kiss
I never expected for life to be like this
Having a woman like you was always my wish

I pray that you are doing well and fine
I had breakfast this morning without my Sunshine
I love you though and I always will
I won't stray from you because I'm on chill

You are the most amazing woman that I know
Besides granny who is cool as the breeze blow
I had to leave in order to find reprieve and breath
I didn't come all the way here just to not believe

I'm remaining strong brave and hopeful
Things of the past don't bother me...so
What will you come up with next
Because I love you way too much to be vexed

Just do you babe and I'll do me
When we're together we do each other see
Mirror mirror on the wall who's the best of em all
The mirror replied to me you're the best sweetie

~Jeffrey Lauriston

Deep Sleep:

Father God I thank you for a good night's rest
Despite my adversities I'm at my best
I had some funny dreams that made me laugh
Father I'm finally getting over things of the past

I also had a great day on yesterday
I got to relax a little and chill with babe
After we chilled I also had a chance to play
By going to the gym not too far from my way

Father Jesus I thank you for my three sons
You've freed us and made us all cham-pi-ons
You gave me chances just to be myself
Now I love me more than I love anyone else

I thank you Lord for your giving me
A chance to grow while living life care free
I learn new things each and everyday
Like not letting anyone make me have a bad day

Dear Lord I thank you for such sound sleep
I mean that sleep was deep I mean real real deep
Now as I'm done praying and rising to my feet
I ask that you help to make all our days complete

~Jeffrey Lauriston

Lost In The Sauce:

I was lost in the sauce
Trying to better gauge my reach
Now I know that at all cost
It is much better for me to teach

Even if I'm not teaching others
I can definitely teach myself
That as sisters and as brothers
We must stand together or else

Life is truly super awesome in my eyes
Though there's been a foggy patch
I would like to sincerely apologize
For giving way for negativity to hatch

We may not realize our own weight
And may not realize our own pull
We must try hard to demonstrate
Ways to promote growth while being cool

By growth I mean to be well rounded
Physically spiritually and mentally fit
What I once lost I have found it
Everything is okay now the flow is legit

I was so lost in the sauce
I can't tell you whether it was barbeque
Yet again I do know that at all cost
I can't stand the thought of losing you

I Love You Cara

~Jeffrey Lauriston

Love Birds:

Father Jesus you're amazing in all you do
I love revere and appreciate you too
You've done everything which you needed to
To keep me afloat and help carry me through

Father Jesus I dance and sing songs for you
There's nothing that I wouldn't do for you
You've given me missions with no end near
Only to help make the path bright and clear

You've taken the lowly and made him your own
Fill him with your glory as you sit on your throne
I love you dear Jesus with all that I have
You turned a blocked Broadway to an open Ave.

You've shown me your mercy your grace and all
And have given me the greatest gifts of them all
Soon I'll be with the greatest treasure throughout
The most Beautiful Queen representing the South

Cara my dearest you make my heart float
I am so proud to have you I show off and I gloat
At the same time I'm humbled by life itself
I want you and you alone and no one else

I Love You Jesus
You Too Cara

~Jeffrey Lauriston

True Love Manifests:

Okay okay okay

We've gone two days with no phone call
I text you and you won't text back at all
I tell you I love you and you say I'm sappy
But when we're making love...you call me Papi

And when we way up you can't stop me
But you're the realest though no imitation copy
I let these feelings grow so I can love you best
I'm getting tired though with all your silly tests

Why can't you see it Yo...True Love Manifests
I let these heavy chains flow right off my chest
We went toe to toe till about round three
That's when your loving came got the best of me

I don't eat chicken things with no sesame
But would really like your wing right next to me
I'm loving what you bring to the table see
You've got an open womb where I can plant a tree

It's been two days seems like twenty thousand
I'm learning every day that no man is an island
I can still be Alpha and remain humble
Not unlike those monks in the Shaolin temples

~Jeffrey Lauriston

Swoon Romance:

All I want you to do is dance dance dance
Come right here baby now here's your chance
Show me what you got yeah they call me Lance
It's not because I Ro but it's because I Romance

All I want you to do is shake shake shake
While you shaking say my heart you wont break
I'm down for the baking so let's bake bake bake
These move you're making are great great great

How much more can you take take take
Remember our evening by the lake lake lake
That's the day I proposed posed posed
The day we dipped our feet and toes toes toes

That night you had me expose pose pose
Why it was you that I chose chose chose
Then I told you quick & in truth truth truth
I chose you because you chose me too too too

What are we ever going to do do do
Can't go another week without you you you
I say dreams are bound to come true true true
Let's see if you dream about me too too too

All I want you to do is dance dance dance
This may be our last chance chance chance
But in truth and in reality there's no such thing
Since even in the end a new beginning can reign

~Jeffrey Lauriston

She's A Diva:

I've been on the other side...of the river
Where the people say Olas
I've got twelve in my quiver
Pressing the world on my shoulders

I've never been a receiver
So I don't catch skin
But I am known to deliver
I'm guaranteed to pull a win

Since I'm not in competition
I always stay winning
Now that Cara is my mission
My winning is never ending

Soon I'll be in perfect position
To go all the way to Venus
She is what I have been missing
She is so good for my fitness

I have been on the other side...of the river
And you wouldn't believe what I've seen
I kept catching glimpses of my Diva
Running all throughout my daydreams

~Jeffrey Lauriston

Sugar & Spice:

I said she was a Diva
But I meant to say Divine
She knows how to deliver
And she delivers on time

She makes it Buena Buena
That's because she makes it good
She raises my antenna
Every time she mentions food

See I'm a demi sexual
And had to get used to her style
But being that she's so special
It only took but a short while

We took it from slow motion
And now we're full speed ahead
I had to cause commotion
So she won't play with my head

The same way I am warm
I could be so very cold
I rather press my charms
Being too cold was getting old

I really love my sugar
And I appreciate my spice
She is my Buggah Wuggah
Lady Supreme so super nice

I said she was a Diva
But I made a big mistake

She made me a believer
That she's a Goddess in my wake

I Love You Cara

~Jeffrey Lauriston

I Love You Manie:

Grandma I love you like no other
I love you like a son loves his mother
I appreciate everything you've done
You taught me how to not be undone

You were there for me early on
And till this day your love still carries on
I remember the first time we went shopping
From then on we've been market hopping

Granny you've got a super cool style
You're so serious all the time...I love your smile
Thank you for sticking strong with the faith
And for always guarding me keeping me safe

I know that these past few years has been tough
Jean used to say Le Pap di enough is enough
Everything is soon to change tides do shift
I am so sorry for all the pain if you catch my drift

Grandma I will love you forever
To stop loving you that will happen never
I love it how you're so smart witty and clever
Pulling pranks left and right like whatever

~Jeffrey Lauriston

Child Of God:

Take a good look in the mirror
Can't you see how beautiful you are
Yes it's true I'm talking to you
You're brilliant just like a star

It's okay to let go of yesterdays
Especially since today will be better anyway
Don't feel sorrow worrying about tomorrow
Enjoy enjoy enjoy because time is borrowed

As for me I will chase love
Because it is in love I find my peace
Which does not mean I do not think of...
Myself in the process I am in love with me

It's just so much love to give
It's concentrated and super strong
It is in God's love and light where I live
And have done so for so very long

When I look in the mirror
Do you know what it is that I see
I see a perfect Child Of God
Standing there staring back at me

~Jeffrey Lauriston

A True Champion:

Good morning Father Jesus how are you
I'm doing fine I hope that you are too
I want to take this time just to thank you
For everything you've done and that you do

You are my greatest hero I'm your biggest fan
I study your work to better know who I am
Jesus you are awesome bodacious and cool
Father you are the only one who truly rules

Jesus I'd like to ask you to protect us all
Help to pick us back up if ever we were to fall
I saw what you did there just the other day
Oh how you sent that angel flying by my way

It is by your authority why we stand strong
We shall praise your name thru hymns & song
You say to us to only trust and to just believe
Father I trust that you will always be there for me

Good morning Dear Jesus wishing you a fine day
Thanks for being there was all I wanted to say
I love you dear Jesus for all You've ever done
You're the greatest Dear Lord my True Champion

~Jeffrey Lauriston

The Right Love:

If I have ever loved you before
I now love you that much more
It's a love that cannot be ignored
Which sums up to infinity times four

I didn't expect Love to walk thru my door
But that's exactly what picked me off the floor
It was & still is a love like none I've known before
A love so good which keeps me wanting more

Cara love why not come meet by the shore
We could hold hands while we explore
Let's lay in the sand we'll laugh and play
While I tell you I love you in all sorts of ways

I just want to be there for you & see your smile
I thank you for being so loyal all the while
You've proven you've got me day in day out
How love is supposed to be without a doubt

If I ever said that I loved you before
Right now I love you even that much more
Your loving Cara is felt right to the core
The kind of love that I have so longed for

~Jeffrey Lauriston

So Happy Together:

Do you remember that time we went to KFC
What ended up happening in that lobby
That's the day I decided that you would be
My brand new favorite and full time hobby

When you left I decided to call your mom
So that she could help me to find you
You got so mad back home you wouldn't come
Till you were convinced that I really did have you

There are other things that we did there and here
That brought us closer together as a couple
I will never forget the night I brought you to tears
That's the night I knew that I was in big trouble

I've spent everyday since trying to right my wrong
I remained unforgiven for God knows how long
It was an error truly a mistake that I can't undo
It will never ever ever happen again I promise you

I won't bring up that day at KFC
Unless it's you who wishes to recall
How it is that you were always there for me
Even when I wasn't there for you at all

I Love You Cara

~Jeffrey Lauriston

Only You:

I only really want you
Because there's only one of me
Why would I want three or two
When you've got all that I need

I did and said things only due
...To the fact that I was sad and hurt
So long as I know your love is true
There's no need for me to have side skirts

In all reality you're more than enough
When we're together we have so much fun
You can't deny that I am your biggest crush
I've proven that I really do love you all along
I've left everything in God's hands
He showed me how to align with His plan
Therefore there are no worries but jubilation
I'm this close to departing from tribulation

In all honesty I can't complain life is great
Imagine how greater it will be if we're straight
Trust understanding & consideration are plenty
To keep one feeling healthy and not empty

It's always only been about you
Then you brought uncertainty through
Why lose true love only to gain lust
We each should be enough for the two of us

~Jeffrey Lauriston

Poetry In Motion:

See me by the horizon
Where the ocean is known to meet the sky
After which It will be mountains
Which we will be perched on...you & I

You really have to start somewhere
Before one can finally reach the top
The secret is that once you get there
...You don't ever look back & do not stop

Right now Cara I will be honest
And tell you that you're all that I need
Yes it is very true your highness
It's indeed by your love I've been set free

They would call it poetry in motion
Yet there'd be no motion if it weren't for you
I would cross over ten thousand oceans
If it meant I'd have a chance to be with you

Ponce De Leon searched for a fountain
Which contained properties to make him young
I myself will never need no such thing
I haven't aged since the day you got me sprung

Come and see me by the horizon
Where new dreams and possibilities may unfold
I'm so glad that you're now in my life when...
There was a time I feared relations where getting old

~Jeffrey Lauriston

Missing You:

You are my best friend
And I say this to you all the time
How you mean the world to me
I'm so fortunate that you're mine

While I'm down here missing you
I am busy occupying my mind
By finding new things to do
I hope that you do miss me too

It was really nice to hear from you
& happy to know things are going well
I've written a few songs for you
It may be more than a few but I won't tell

There's nothing sweeter than your voice
Which sounds just like music to my ears
What's even sweeter is kissing your lips
Especially when it helps to ease your fears

You've always been my best friend
I appreciate you more and more each day
You're someone upon who I can depend
I'm more than happy God sent you my way

~Jeffrey Lauriston

Future Past:

Cara you are my first and my last
You're my present and future past
You are my mountain top & ocean floor
I dream of walking through your door

I could never come to love you too much
Because too much is simply not enough
I always ask of you through secret posts
For you to tell me who really loves you most

I didn't start to live again until you revived me
As I was going through it all you stood by me
We have lots of fun together when we're free
It's funny how in everything it is you that I see

I just want to be your one & only Cherry Tree
Be my Mother Earth & come cultivate with me
Cara love of all loves & dearest of all dearests
This love that I have for you is something serious

Maybe I haven't told you you're my last & first
The only one who could have quenched my thirst
The greatest gifts to be had is to be found in you
God helping us to produce another baby or two

~Jeffrey Lauriston

Wishy Washy:

Sweet Cara my dearest love of all loves
Don't you know it's you who I think of
What's this I hear about you having doubts
When you already know what my love is all about

I told you that you're more than just a flame
Why do you think I'm willing to give you my name
You're extraordinarily super terrific and you're rare
You and I will come to make the most perfect pair

That term wishy washy has been used a lot
We should have gone to Hibachi but I plum forgot
Despite all of that girl you are all I've got
Cara you keep me sweating because you're so hot

I'll keep on complimenting until the day I die
You're the one that I want and if you ask me why
I'll say because I love you more that you'll ever know
Can't wait to plug one in you so I can see that glow

My sweetie Cara Dove dearest love of all loves
I'm glad you've got my back come shove and shove
You're more than super sexy oh how I love you so
Just let me be your Nestle letting the chocolate flow

~Jeffrey Lauriston

I Love You Jesus:

Father God I come to praise your name
Since I've accepted Jesus my life isn't the same
I thought that down was up and up was down
Just a lost soul left wondering around town

Lord Jesus came to my rescue countless times
He gave me a voice where I once was a mime
Lord God gave me the courage to be myself
And to be in great physical and spiritual health

Father Jesus you are awesome & totally rad
You are the best friend I've ever had
I could never love you as much as you love me
But will sincerely try to give you the best of me

Father God you are my all my refuge and heart
I love you so much for giving me a new start
Sometimes it's hard for me to let go of the old
Yet in your love I have learned how to be bold

I love you I love you I love you I love you
Dear Father Jesus oh how I really do
You're my everything you being my all
Who is ever present when his name is called

I Love You Lord Jesus

~Jeffrey Lauriston

Pretty Princess:

She's a dime though she really is a quarter
The ninety nine to my penny to make a dollar
Man she so fine that my line is out of order
This isn't Taco Bell but I'm headed for the border

In my life I've yet to meet one bolder
A pretty princess with long legs & nice shoulders
She peeked my interest from first I had laid eyes
And till this day she still has me so mesmerized

Said she's a quarter but she keeps it one hundred
She has a project best believe that I'll fund it
In my life she's exactly what I've been missing
And she might be the best cook up in the kitchen

When she harkens most people pay attention
No sky larking to bring about any apprehension
She's my main dish including all of the fixins
And to love her is my one and only mission

She's a dime but really more like a half dollar
Now she's mine & got me feeling like a scholar
I was short but bcuz of her I feel much taller
& for sports I hope to have a new son or daughter

~Jeffrey Lauriston

Teachings:

It's quite okay to be yourself
And not be like everybody else
You can come to forge your own identity
You being you and not necessarily like me

Figure out what it is that you can do
Then make sure that you do it often & well
And if someone wishes to be like you
Be sure to show them better than you can tell

If it is for an example that they search
Be that example while maintaining your worth
If it is answers that they wish to find
Be then the solution so that they are not blind

You're a problem solver who knows how to think
Your breakthrough is coming you're on the brink
Keep on pressing forward while moving along
Bcuz you're heading towards a brand new song

There is never a wrong way for you to do right
Nor is there a right way for you to ever do wrong
Though I am finally merging with the good light
This journey of ours is still so very long

That's why I say just to be you for true
Cuz at the end of the day there's none like you
Just stay positive trying to live and let live
Most important of all always be willing to give

~Jeffrey Lauriston

Beautiful Journey:

Sometimes you may have to break yourself down
Only so that you can build yourself back up
Sometimes you have to act like a complete clown
So that your crown will straighten its act up

People will always be quick to take advandtage
If you were not to draw for them a bold line
As if compassion were a foreign language
Most of the time it's me mine mine mine

This life of ours could be a beautiful journey
...Of self discovery and so much more
As I'm learning you I expect for you to learn me
That's mostly why we're in each other's lives for

See how Christ loves the church with a passion
That's also how passionate I really am about you
It's for open communication and trust I'm asking
I promise that I will provide the same to you too

The reason I hung tough is because you've shown
...That you actually really do care for me
It's funny how I'm older but you're more grown
And I had to quickly catch up to your maturity

When it comes to you I have to place you first
That's what a real man is supposed to do tis all
Thankfully God has gotten us through the worst
We may have stumbled a bit but we did not fall

Sometimes you may have to break yourself down
Because the way to the top is such a fun ride
We'll get things right this second time around
As I'm very certain that you'll soon be my bride

~Jeffrey Lauriston

A Very Special Lady:

Have you ever met someone
You never wanted to go a day without
That very special someone
You spend a lifetime figuring out

That person who you can talk to
Without fear of ever being judged
The one who will go all out for you
Who's love is permanent and won't budge

I have met a special lady
Who's been in my life now for a while
Sometimes I would call her baby
Just so that I could get to make her smile

I told her what was in a name
And just how much she means to me
We figured we both want the same thing
Which is a lasting bond in unity

Have you ever met an angel
Who never cared to expose their wings
My life went from being all mangled
To now my having just about everything

I wrote this so that I could thank her
For bringing love in my direction
She's my left right front and center
Indeed the main cause for my affection

I Love You Cara

~Jeffery Lauriston

Skyfall:

Can you hear me when I am calling
Can you see exactly what I'm trying to say
You alone are my one and only darling
And I truthfully wouldn't have it any other way

You're not feeling so well right now
And sadly I am nowhere around
Yet I am very confident that somehow
A true lasting remedy is soon to be found

Last night all of my dreams consisted of you
Wherein it seems there was more than us two
In the distance I heard the faint sounds of coos
And the singing of lullabies with I love yous

Your sweetness is my weakness & cuteness too
As God is my witness there's much I long to do
Like love you protect you and care for you
While being able to dutifully provide for you too

You truly are more than just a dream come true
Everything that I need is to be found within you
I love you more and more with each new day
& not worried anymore whether or not you'll stay

Can you see me when I am calling
Can you feel what it is I say
Our dear skies are no longer falling
Everything will soon be okay

~Jeffrey Lauriston

New Life:

What greater joy is there...
Than to create bringing forth new life
Especially if you're a pair
I'm referring to being husband & wife

And just how much better would it be
Knowing that we are doing what God wants
Imagine all of the wonderful blessings we
....Will get to enjoy as a God fearing family

I respect love and only wish to honor you
Not to punish but to care for and cherish you
Life's exchanges however should be reciprocal
When fairness is in play resentments are minimal

When I say that I love you & that you're beautiful
I mean to also add there's none more suitable
To have and to hold until forever and more
Watching as miracles unfold like never before

What greater joy could there be...
Than that of being with family
Though views are abstract I can clearly see
That you're in fact the one who God made for me

~Jeffrey Lauriston

Time To Celebrate!:

I had a really good time today
Chilling with fam and everything
I allowed myself to laugh dance & play
Even though I say that I play no games

Life is all about finding balance
You can't be too left or too right
When I'm all alone and in sheer silence
Is when I can best see God's good light

I'm so grateful and I'm very appreciative
For all the great things which God has done
He has given me a chance to once again live
May even bless me with a new daughter or son

He has given me someone who I can count on
She has been there throughout it all
I've found in Cara a true & faithful companion
My beauty queen there to keep me standing tall

I had one of the greatest times ever today
Even though my queen isn't yet around
Today happens to be our anniversary anyway
A wonderful celebration is very soon to be found

~Jeffrey Lauriston

My Prerogative:

Here we go again for yet another round
I went up before standing pound for pound
I waited on my girl before I came back down
At first I was lost now my destination is found

I know at all cost I have to stand my ground
& that she's my prerogative like Bobby Brown
So I will be sticking to my onus & doing my job
It's my job to protect her & not to make her sob

Cara please forgive me for all that I've done
Despite any differences I still love you a ton
As I look into your eyes and I see a Champion
You're my one and only being my number one

At the same time though do not cross the line
What's mine is yours and what's yours is mine
With Christ in our lives everything will be fine
We won't bring up those numbers six or nine

Here we go again now that the bell has just rung
Okay I will admit Cara that you've got me sprung
I get high off of your loving like Cheech & Chung
It's right in your oven where I will bake a bun

~Jeffrey Lauriston

Open Book:

Everywhere that I turn
It is your beautiful face I see
As we live and we learn
We churn closer towards our destiny

What is to be found
Is God's promise of the crown
Be ye not dismayed
All will be well because we prayed

It is in our Lord
Where inspiration is to be had
Living in one accord
Will guarantee that we will be glad

It is in the light where I choose to live
As I learn to live I'm learning to let live
Though we may not do all things right
We can learn how to rightly forgive

Don't be easily fooled & don't be schooled
By those who do not really care about you
Some will use and lose you like a tool
Being used to be discarded is never cool

Everywhere I turn and I look
I see your smiling face next to me
And just likened to a beautiful open book
It'll be more chapters which we shall see

~Jeffery Lauriston

Sailing The Sky:

If I were ever to sing you a song
I would tell you just how much
That I desire and do so long
To feel the softness of your touch

I would mention your bright smile
And how it lights up my whole life
And I would tell you all the while
How you're my earthly paradise

As I come to taste your lips
My heart will be filled with delight
Dearest Love I have to grip
And hold on to you really tight

You say that there are three suns
Which compliments our three moons
Though I call you Star just for fun
You will be a star pretty soon

If it were a ballad that I wrote
It would touch upon your sweet grace
I'd then soar while I sail & float
Towards your nice pretty little face

~Jeffrey Lauriston

Trust God:

One day at a time
That is how we'll get by
One day at a time
All we have to do is just try

One bite at a time
Until we clear out our plate
A peaceful state of mind
Is something to appreciate

One second by the hour
All we must do is breath
And take heed to God's power
Please be ye not deceived

Life is bound to still go on
Even well after we're gone
You are never truly alone
God is peering from his throne

One day at a time
Just always give it your best
You will then come to find
That you really are truly blessed

As you walk on by
I can see greatness in you
Remember not to cry
When Jesus carries you thru

~Jeffrey Lauriston

We Shall See:

I'm sitting underneath a mango tree
While being as happy as can be
It looks like my girl is back with me
Who's favorite quote is "We Shall See"

I'm not gonna lie I love this girl a lot
At times she gets me mad I mean real hot
Yet no matter what she does I still care
I just have to teach her how not to go there

I got the chance to meet her entire family
& what's funny is they were all digging me
I'm not sure what she did to steal my heart
It may be due to the fact that she's smart

Not a day passes by without thinking of her
I told her from the onset that she's my cure
She really helped to mend a broken heart
Though it's this same heart she tore apart

The bible says to walk by faith & not sight
That means I know I'm safe & all is alright
I could be soft but I'm still a freaking man
Don't set me off then say Oh I'm just playin

I love you baby doll you know I really do
That is the reason why I am coming for you
When I get there baby you better act right
Cuz If you don't I'll be gone the same night

As I sit under this splendid mango tree
I thank God for all that he has done for me
I swear that her & I are really meant to be
Like she says all the time "We Shall See"

~Jeffrey Lauriston

The Double Edged Sword:

I did not want it to be this way
But you refuse to get your life on track
You have rebuttals for everything I say
Now you're asking for me to come back

I will go ahead and make the trip
But don't try to play with me not one bit
I'm cool calm & kind for a really good reason
Keeping a peace of mind throughout the seasons

I don't understand who conditioned your mind
To think that what you're doing is dandy & fine
I've already told you that Jesus is the light
Surrender yourself to him & all will be alright

You've been through a lot of crap in your life
I'm still willing & ready to make you my wife
Just because I love you doesn't mean I'm weird
Seems my thinking of you has got you scared

I've been put through a lot of different stages
Them thinking I was one to be up in cages
It's messed up when you're prejudged by some
Who makes you feel unwanted & unwelcome

The past is the past come & lets move forward
I care about you baby and Love is our reward
See that tongue of yours is a two edge sword
Losing your cool and stuff that you can't afford

I really didn't want things to be this way
I refuse to see your life in ruins and in decay
I do not have a cape so I can't save them all
I'm willing to help you stand in case you fall

~Jeffrey Lauriston

Buttercup:

I met a very beautiful woman the other day
Who asked if I wanted to go out & play
At first I really didn't know what to say
Until she said to me you have to pay to play

I looked her up & down before I said no way
A classy guy like me doesn't have to pay
If anything it should be the other way around
But that is not how I prefer to get down

I'd rather have what's called an even exchange
That's when she started to act all strange
As if what I was saying was foreign to her
I said look just let me make your kitty cat purr

All of the sudden there protruded a sly smile
She said you've got a point & a real nice style
I said okay alright since we see eye to eye
We will go out tonight...besides you're mad fly

I promise you that we had the best time ever
She had on a cat suit & the suit was leather
I was having a bad day and was like whatever
Until that fateful night where it all got better

I then said to her can I ask you a question
Why did you choose hooking as your profession
That night I learned from her a valuable lesson
Realized how important it is counting blessings

She told me about her past how tough it was
How she would get abused by her favorite cuz
Her father wasn't there when she was young
Then she met a pimp who got her sprung

This dude she met had her on all types of stuff
I asked her to tell me when enough was enough
She got so accustomed to how things are
She couldn't see her beauty & that she's a star

I decided to tell her all it was that I saw
How I thought she was amazing very sexy & raw
Then I saw the tears flowing down her cheeks
& since that night we've been chilling for weeks

I'm trying to give her a semblance of a normal life
Hoping that one day she'll be someone's wife
She went & applied getting accepted to school
She now attends Devry and everything is cool

She said to me just now that she wants more
And wouldn't like to see me walk out of her door
That's when I told her Baby we're just friends
But that doesn't mean our friendship has to end

She leaped off of her bed to come give me a hug
I kissed her forehead then said that's what's up
She said that all her life she's only dated thugs
And said I was the first to call her Buttercup

I'm very happy to see my friend is on her way
She's not out walking the streets just to get pay
She tells me how she's grateful every other day
I'm just glad that she's alright & that she's okay

~Jeffrey Lauriston

Ocean Breeze:

Seems like today I got me a win
My friend sure knows how to represent
I know that I maybe shouldn't have gone in
But it is still in where I've gone and went

I should've just walked along her shores
Before deciding that I'd dive in
It felt refreshing though...right to the core
Being able to paddle and stroke within

Today turned out to be really nice
Getting to taste the fine Ocean Breeze
It really felt like I was in paradise
Able to feel like I can finally breath

I then swam my way up to her river banks
That's when the rapids began to churn
The river said to me Hey Jeffrey thanks
...for allowing me the chance to get a turn

I told the river that Twas no prob
Because clearing channels is what I do
I do it really well indeed I do a fine job
And then decided to thank the river too

Today I can say I definitely had a big win
Having my bald head free flow in the wind
I left my friend girl with a nice grin on her chin
And says that she can't wait to do it all again

~Jeffrey Lauriston

Up To No Good:

I just received an important phone call
From a woman of which I gave my all
She was someone I thought I knew for sure
Thought this woman was wholesome & pure

She asked why I was so disappointed for
Trying hard to get me disjointed some more
Piecing together the fragments of my life
Was her only one onus as my future wife

Seems like she doesn't know just where to turn
I reminded her that respect isn't given but earned
She knew before when she betrayed my trust
Having to tell her she shouldn't work against us

I'm going all out to make sure that she's good
Only to find out that she was up to no good
I think it best if I were to just leave her alone
I tried to work with her to build a stable home

She would much rather lie & do me wrong
I've done my best to help to keep her strong
She once assured me that I'd be her only one
Only to turn around & break my heart for fun

I just now received a disturbing phone call
One which I wish I did not answer at all
I swear she's trying to drive me up the wall
Determined and working hard to see me fall

~Jeffrey Lauriston

The Eighth Wonder:

How many ways can I tell you Cara
That you amaze & that you're a wonder
A classy woman who's filled with thunder
Coming to my rescue when I was under

Guess I'll start off with your lovely smile
Before commenting on your sexy style
You should come by and chill for a while
I'll tell you tales about the River Nile

I'll tell you stories about Osiris and Seth
& how there's not too many like you left
Reveal how Isis put him back together
& how your niceness makes me better

Did I forget to say that you are a queen
Probably the most beautiful I have seen
This should not come to you as a surprise
How your beauty keeps men mystified

What if I were to tell you that you're a gem
Would you mind going out with me then
& by gem I mean a diamond or a ruby
Let me in to better fulfill my duty

How many ways can tell you Cara
That you are The World's Eighth Wonder
You are so virtuous & full of grace
Possessing a beauty that can't be replaced

~Jeffrey Lauriston

The 3 Wise Men:

Babe what I wouldn't give to be with you
Even if it's only for an hour or two
Come sit next to me up under the stars
I will point out to you Vega Orion & Mars

Let me hold you for a little while
Let me kiss you gently on your neck
I know you might bruise easily child
But I love you so what the heck

I promise I wasn't trying to dodge yah
Looking all super charged like a Charger
If you slip away how am I gonna find yah
Why can't you see that your love is a factor

I've proven by my actions that I've gotcha
Please don't give me reasons to doubt yah
Evoke more reasons for me to love yah
So that this love of ours will last forever

This isn't the jungle I'm not flushed with fever
However by being humble I'm now a believer
I tried calling & you didn't pick up the receiver
Now you're falling becuz I left like Quick Silver

I don't mind if I have to be a Lone Ranger
So long as I can guard you from danger
Don't you ever dare treat me like a stranger
The 3 Wise Men will be visiting our manger

Babe what I wouldn't give to be with you
To live out our lives and to build with you
Please do not take me for an imbecile
Then I will be forced to see the fool in you

~Jeffrey Lauriston

Cold As Ice:

She said to me that she needed more ice
I said that I liked things a bit more tepid
Being too cold isn't at all that nice
Your frigid nature girl I really detest it

I love a woman who's sweet and kind
Someone who's cool sexy & proper
I would rather have me a peace of mind
Preferring a beauty designed to capture

Not everything you want you get
Though my God hasn't failed me yet
Right now my life is straight & proper set
It has been that way since the day we met

I'm sure soon you'll be on the same page
We finally let the bird up out of its cage
I've done enough to you to get you enraged
Yet no matter what happens you play a sage

She asked for me to be as cold as ice
I said to her I will instead warm it up twice
She's not only mad because I'm too polite
But also very sad because I treat her right

~Jeffrey Lauriston

Mount Zion:

It's a dog eat dog world
I am so glad that I'm a lion
I can't wait to go meet my girl
Right off of Mount Zion

She's a special kind of woman
Who knows how to steal hearts
And she has got my heart wide open
Because she is such a sweetheart

It's a dog eat dog world
Lucky for me I like fish
But this one here is a pearl
Who doesn't clam up when kissed

Oh yeah she is a rock star
The one who lights up my night sky
Though right now she is a bit far
It isn't too far for me to drive or fly

In this crazy world of ours
Where dogs like to take bites
I would much rather go on a tour
Making sure that my girl is alright

When we're back in our own bubble
I'll be more apt to do more
Like keeping her guarded from trouble
Since I'll be right there with her for sure

~Jeffrey Lauriston

True Masterpiece:

Cara it is your loving
Which I long for the most
You are sweeter than a muffin
And tastier than Stove Top stuffing

I looked in to those eyes of yours
And then I just completely froze
Your canvas is so fun to tour
I would like to paint on it some more

I really love it how my bristles
Leaves such a masterful touch
You don't have to blow my whistle
In order to enjoy strokes from my brush

Priceless are all the artwork
That you and I come to produce
They are definitely not of this earth
Being as majestic as Hera and Zeus

Cara it is your loving
And yours alone that I really need
To ask for more my dear sweet darling
Would be a clear sign of sheer greed

~Jeffrey Lauriston

Light As A Feather:

Life is so amazing
I mean it is wonderfully great
God has managed to set things straight
It's getting close for time to celebrate

Yet every day is a celebration
What a joy it is to love and live
My heart remains filled with jubilation
I'm left with no choice but to stay positive

While in this perpetual state of bliss
Call it Nirvana or whatever that you wish
I'll develop ways to do share my joy with others
Besides we're all considered sisters and brothers

There is so much more to be discovered
I love seeing how the magic is to unfold
Don't go around destroying one another
We all are worth far more than diamonds & gold

From where I'm standing life is so darn grand
Let us all begin to unite and overstand
We can do a lot more when joined together
Being stiff as a board & as light as a feather

~Jeffrey Lauriston

You're The Best:

I find it so hard to get you out of my mind
Hope the feeling is mutual I shall know in time
I just want a future with you Sweet Clamentine
I just wanna be there for you come rain or shine

This morning I tried to get you on the phone line
To remind you that you are an angel of mine
If it were not for your grace and loving embrace
Sure Jah wouldn't continue to bless this place

Can't reach you thru a dial tone I will thru text
And tell you not to worry because we're next
We're next in line for blessings and success
Oh did I forget to mention that You're Da Best

Twenty million I love yous will never ever show
How much you are valued from your head to toe
I rather speak through actions so to show I care
You'll have the satisfaction of knowing I'm there

I find it so hard to keep from thinking about you
This has only happened maybe once before you
Exquisite is the word I will use to describe you
I hope my visit will prove my love is tried & true

~Jeffrey Lauriston

Blessed:

I am too blessed to be stressed
Got so much that I can't think less
Everyday is another great gift
Thank you Lord for not letting me drift

I am driven and plan to count on you
Very forgiving only because you are too
Thanks for the opportunities you provide
You've yet to ever fail me being my guide

You taught me it's you alone I should trust
& that I'm not on my own being there for us
Where ever you send me Lord is where I'll go
You're my shield my sword & I love you so

Lifted me right off my back to head to you
Helped to keep me all intact as usual
I fear not for I do serve such a great God
Giving me all I deserve Lord that says a lot

I am way too blessed to ever be stressed
Whatever I ask of God He always says yes
It is such a great joy getting to live this life
& thank you from my heart for your sacrifice

~ Jeffrey Lauriston

Free Flow:

I saw the big picture
Suddenly life became clear
It is a permanent fixture
That I shall make you my dear

Why have you in my life
For just a temporary stay
I could instead make you my wife
For forever with added days

I can come peer into your eyes
And tell you all that you mean
It should not come as a surprise
When I refer to you as queen

I would like to hold you in my arms
To keep you real warm nice and safe
I won't be the one to do you harm
Nor will I ever dirty your face

The first time didn't go as planned
Let's see this time how things will flow
Like Custard I am willing to take a stand
At the end of the aisle I will take your hand

I saw the big picture
And now have come to realize
That by you being part of the mixture
It will be much easier to sail the skies

~ Jeffrey Lauriston

Love You Still:

How is it possible
That I still love you girl
Being so inhospitable
While you were up in my world

Your love was criminal
And really not that smooth
Message subliminal
There is nothing left to prove

You put me through the ringer
For many years on end
I would give you the finger
But I'll reserve that for a friend

The more that things change
The more they stay the same
Why are you acting strange
When you are the one to blame

You tried to take me out
For no reason at all
Showed you what I'm about
With Christ it's hard for me to fall

We both could still be civil
If that is what you would like
You let them all deceive you
Let them fill your head with hype

No need to worry girl
I've got no hate for you
You're still a precious pearl
And always will be beautiful

Irma just passed on through
So we can start off fresh
I hold no grudge for you
Always hoping you be blessed

I once was petrified
Now I'm cool as the breeze
Just can't believe my eyes
Seeing what God has done for me

It's very possible
For me to love you still
While highly probable
The truth will come to be revealed

~Jeffrey Lauriston

Proud & Tall:

How great is our nation
This land of the free
You'll come for a vacation
& this is where you'd want to be

It's beyond being patriotic
It's having true love for your home
The United States of America
...Is where I am from

How great it is to...
Live in a democracy
I don't know about you
...But that's great to me

We have freedom of speech
But that is not all
Due to our country's reach
We can stand proud and tall

Oh how I do love
...the great U.S. of A.
And I can't think of
Anywhere else I'd rather stay

My fifty stared flag
With it's red white and blue
Always seems to make me glad
& you should be happy too

How magnificent is this...
Our country of brotherly love
Whether by air land or sea
The U.S. of A. will rise above

~Jeffrey Lauriston

Fairy Tales:

I could easily be your Romeo
But you can't be my Juliette
Because in this here fine rodeo
I wouldn't want you to go just yet

We shall not commit atrocious acts
All in the sacred name of love
Because we both know that love in fact
Is something that can sustain both of us

You could also be my Cinderella
And I could be that charming dude
Won't claim to be a noble fella
There are times I know I'm just too rude

I can't think of any other fairy tales
That could be synonymous to me & you
If there's one thing that I can say & tell
It's that I've yet to meet a girl like you

I really wouldn't mind being your Romeo
But you have to understand I can't let go
If you wish I can simply be your Lothario
That way we can continue on with our flow

~Jeffrey Lauriston

Soul Mate:

How many ways can I possibly say it
I really do not know
I do however know how to display it
I can't tell as well as I can show

Before this I wrote about five reasons
Which had to be done during hurricane season
I left you in sheer disbelief
Never imagining mine would be the face you see

Woman you've got power and virtue
I will never do anything that will hurt you
This morning despite the warnings & curfew
I still decided to drive over just to see you

I would like to let you know you're the greatest
Loving how you pay no mind to the haters
On this end...everything is buenos
It's a full house and I'm not even John Stamos

I wonder how many ways I can come to say
That I love you lots...baby baby (in Biggie's voice)
I don't want this love of ours to ever go away
That's why I pray every day for our love to stay

~Jeffrey Lauriston

Five Reasons Why:

Just give me one reason
& I'll promise to give you four
Why is it that I love you
More and more & more

This is the very season
Which our God has had in store
He's surely going to bless you
Like you've never been blessed before

Though you've yet to go
I'll start with reason number one
You are super duper beautiful
& for that alone I love you a ton

Please do give me a few
To come up with reason number two
Oh yeah that's right It's true
Someday I plan to marry you

Now that I am finally free
Here is my reason number three
I keep on falling deeper for thee
Because you are just so good to me

Wait there is still one more
So here we are with reason number four
My love for you is from the core
Because you picked me up off the floor

And if ever you were to wish
I would gladly give you a fifth
My lady love you are my favorite gift
One I could see me spending my life with

~Jeffrey Lauriston

Honey Hill:

You are a Daffodil
Upon a honey hill
I like your sex appeal
& love the way you make me feel

I like that you stay real
You're filled with so much zeal
It is such a courtesy
Having you here flirt with me

The sweetness on your lips
And beauty in your eyes
Could make a grown man trip
For that I apologize

If am wrong am wrong
I'm prone to make mistakes
Since you're my favorite song
I promise your heart not to break

I've been a big buffoon
For staying out till noon
I should have came back home
It's you I should've come running to

Got lost deep in her arms
& fell for her warm charms
I should have just said no
But she wouldn't let me go

Forgive me I have sinned
Will you please let me in
What had just happened then
I promise won't occur again

You are my Daffodil
Whose nectar is honey filled
It is with much appeal
I ask that you don't break the seal

~Jeffrey Lauriston

Sacred Love:

Sweet dearest love of all my loves
You were a diamond in the rough
Just as predicted and sure enough
You're super beautiful strong and tough

I cannot stand to have you gone
You being so very far away from me
I'm here trying to weather out this storm alone
When you should be right here next to me

Last night you called me on my mobile phone
Just to make sure that everything was alright
And love when I heard your sweet voices tone
My heart began to flutter with sheer delight

We've had our speed tables on the road
On the road we'll come to call Sacred Love
We both had plenty of reasons to explode
It never came down to being pushed or shoved

There's no use saying how much I miss you
Since there is nothing I can do to change things
We both now realize what is the major issue
But I won't let issues make me do strange things

My love of all loves so tender and oh so sweet
Yours is the best sound to ever bless my ears
Dearest of all dearest you make my life complete
& help me stand erect dissolving all of my fears

~Jeffrey Lauriston

The Day We Met:

I say we should weather this storm together
You and me kiddo we can get thru whatever
What's fast approaching is known as the header
After the eye and tail passes it all will be better

It is one love it's one nation and one heart
That will prevent us from being torn all apart
We have to just let go letting God do his thing
Because in the end he is who reigns supreme

Prayers goes out to everyone in Irma's wake
No matter what transpires our spirits won't break
See it's Jah's Fire that causes the earth to quake
He is the same one who these storms him make

I pray we're all with family and our closest friends
I guess we'll touch bases when this storm ends
There's safety precautions we should adhere to
So please do take caution you are important too

We should come to weather this storm together
I still have not forgotten the day when I met her
Now that she's in my life all will be much better
Now that she's in my life I will love her forever

~Jeffrey Lauriston

Love Letter:

Baby love with all of this pouring rain
Please do not make me wait in vain
I've been trying to show you I'm not playing
Your love drives me wildly crazy my lady

I gave you some good times while together
And actually think we make each other better
I'm this close to calling you a trend setter
You being so sweet and all plus so tender

I'm only human too that's what I've been saying
I also require some assistance like the next man
Hey I come thru whenever I can however I can
I'm not asking you to be my biggest fan

Bet you'd never guess that I was a fan of yours
Seeing how you choose to keep your heart pure
That's love unyielding in its truest form
Something extraordinary and out of the norm

My love dearest with such inclement weather
Why not let me to compose for you a love letter
Hope these melodic tones touch your heart
So that from your love I will never part

~Jeffrey Lauriston

Rise of Champions:

We rise from the ashes
We rise to become and do more
We must heal the masses
What is all the bickering for

I love you like you're my own
Why don't you please lower your tone
Why shouldn't we seek out peace
Amongst our brothers North South West East

Come together as we unite as one
We shall call it the Rise of Champions
Only because that's what we all are in truth
We were winners even while as youths

Seek out to help out one another
Instead of trying to destroy each other
Where is the joy in hurting my brother
Even if we don't have the same mother

We all come from the same father
He is our Heavenly Father
Come at me sideways please don't bother
Tis peace love unity and trust I rather

Oh Oh Oh Oh Oh Oh Oh Well

~Jeffrey Lauriston

Satisfied:

Girl I loved you
But you decided to play
I implored you
Refusing to come my way

Now you're calling
Saying that you made a mistake
So sorry darling
Another heart break I can't take

I can't trust you
With my emotions at all
I adored you
But you'd much rather see me fall

Did the best I...
Knew how to do as your man
Nonetheless I...
Just couldn't keep you from straying

Oh you didn't know
That everything was revealed
But it's okay though
Least I could say my love was real

& with that I'm satisfied
Because I really went hard in the paint
Thought you were bona-fide
Then quickly learned that you just ain't

The more I loved you
You decided that you'd love me less
With all I've been through
I didn't have anytime for your mess

~Jeffrey Lauriston

Far Far Away:

You see me I don't like to chase women
And I really don't mind being around them
To put it simply there are bigger fish to fry
Then just watching as my life passes me by

In this world there is nothing guaranteed
We simply have to be the best that we can be
If you just try there's a good chance you'll succeed
Doing all you can so to live life successfully

There's opposition everywhere that you turn
But that's okay because we live and we learn
The fire blazes hotta hotta as it burns
As we are quickened we know how to discern

Not everything you see is what it really is
That's why it's better to do good being positive
We've been let down too many times in our lives
Just have to strive to keep the faith and hope alive

You see me I am content with who I've become
I'm learning how to let go and how to live some
I was afraid to go out into this vast world
But I can't stand being so far away from my girl

~Jeffrey Lauriston

Magic City:

Gosh I love my city
Called Miami called Miami
And it's in Carol City
Where you'll find me where you'll find me

You'll have to forgive me
I beg your pardon beg your pardon
There's no more Carol City
It's now Miami Gardens Miami Gardens

Miami is the place where I was born I was born
A city of lights that has it going on going on
It's a melting pot here where I come from
It's funny how everybody gets along gets along

There are many who are from the Caribbean
And plenty people who are European
My mother and my father are both Haitian
Would you believe my first son is part Jamaican

Lord protect my city
Called Miami called Miami
Please Lord show some pity
And get behind me get behind me

Here comes hurricane Irma
Trying to steal our magic steal our magic
Don't let Irma's trip to Florida
Be too tragic cause we just won't have it

~Jeffery Lauriston

Come Over:

She asked me to come over
But then decided to ask her why
She said I've got something to show you
So why don't you please just come on by

I said if I come over are you going to let me in
Said to me I will & I want you to meet my friend
I drove on to her house with the widest of grins
Went knocking on her door till I couldn't any more

I got into my car and I was ready to leave
Before she pulled up in a nice red pickup truck
Said see Jeff I do not have tricks up my sleeve
Twas the sound of relief & felt like I could breath

She stayed true to her word & shared her space
I felt free as a bird with a smile on my face
While in my haste I didn't get a chance to taste
But I know next time to just slow up the pace

She text me to come over
And at first did not reply
I then placed her on my shoulders
Before having a real good time

~Jeffrey Lauriston

Great Gifts:

You were my air when I
...Could not breath
It is so hard to believe
That you are still here with me

You made things easier to bear
Being there showing that you care
You are the air that I breath
...That you must believe

I see your smile when I wake
And I think to myself how great
How wonderful it is to have such a gift
Meant to inspire encourage and uplift

I would like to apologize a million times
For the grime and dirt that flew in my eyes
I can see now and are no longer blind
You are awesome for being so kind

You were and still are my air
Whenever I call you're right there
My love for you I swear cannot compare
For this is the truth...refute it I dare

~Jeffrey Lauriston

Solid Rock:

I'm so tired of self sabotaging
Being too afraid to actually succeed
Guess it's time to expand my horizons
To be of more help to those who are in need

Stopping myself from becoming better
Is very selfish of me and now this I know
How will I ever be truly able to protect her
If I do not provide for her a place to go

I have wasted more than enough time
With theories suppositions hypotheses & such
I cannot afford to lose my Dime
Because she is mad fly and I love her so much

I admit that I have been a bit frustrated
Seeing as how I cannot yet give her the world
Don't you worry love for soon we'll make it
Thanks for sticking by me & for being my girl

Self sabotaging is what I like to do most
But all that has to stop to be solid as a rock
I love you babe from this & to the next coast
You're the reason why I long to reach the top

~Jeffrey Lauriston

Ones & Twos

Love how are you doing today
You do know that I miss you right
Sorry things didn't really go our way
But I think you're well worth the fight

I didn't believe in second chances
Until I began making mistakes after mistakes
You were there when I hopped the fences
Never intending for your heart to break

I have wronged you in ways I shouldn't
And to forgive me you simply couldn't
Yes you made me pay and I felt it
I should have eaten it because I dealt it

My love for you goes beyond the sky
Babe I'm so sorry & would like to apologize
I've failed you what seems like countless times
I betrayed your trust so you betrayed mine

I get it and I understand completely
I resign to the fact that you help complete me
I'll spend a lifetime trying to make it up to you
Hope I'm forgiven since I have forgiven you

Love I wanted to know how you were doing
We're not going to watch our union go to ruins
Fight fight fight fight fight like we're the Bruins
We're bobbing & weaving on our ones and twos n'

~Jeffrey Lauriston

Let Me In:

No it's not everyday
I meet someone like you
That smile right on your face
Tells me you like me too

I want to take you out
For a night out on town
Show you what I'm about
And how I do get down

We'll do amazing things
Having us lots of fun
Its so much joy you bring
When out on our one on ones

You take me to places
Where I have never been
At first I didn't know
If you would ever let me in

And now that I'm inside
We went out for some rides
Having you by my side
Makes me feel so alive

I was just taking time
To let you know you're loved
You're my own paradise
Sent from our God up above

~Jeffery Lauriston

Conquering Lion:

We are soldiers in God's army
He protects us and our families
Jah is love and is our salvation
We ask Jesus to bless our nation

Our battalion fights for honor
Our medallions says hallelujah
With Jah's presence I'm no loner
He's my sole reference & my donor

We keep fighting for Jah's glory
No back biting...end of story
Jah we love you for forever
You have caused us to get better

Jesus you are our true lifeline
You have been there thru our life time
Sweet Jehovah who's up in Zion
You're the one true Conquering Lion

We are soldiers in God's army
We are soldiers in Jah's army
You have cared for & loved us plenty
It's by the sea shore you gave us entry

We are soldiers in God's army

~Jeffrey Lauriston

Day & Night:

Don't no body ever gotta know
It'll just be between me and you
What we do won't ever be for show
They're not gonna see me loving you

I am known as Mr. Lover Optimal
By my lady friends near where I live
They help to make life more beautiful
By all the sweet loving that they all give

I'm just saying that if you are in need
Of a little relaxation underneath our sun
Then it really wouldn't be a thing for me
To take you out for a day & night of fun

I'll tell you to lay back and close your eyes
Just to help take your cares & stresses away
There will not be any need for alibis
Cause he won't even know that you were away

Don't nobody even have to ever know
That we've composed some classics in our time
We've separated the truth away from the show
& they'll never have to know that you are mine

~Jeffrey Lauriston

Forever My Always:

You are to be my lady
For forever and and for a lifetime
Don't try and drive me crazy
Just because they say love is blind

Why don't we take a stab...
At this love thing one more time
So that we both can dab
On any haters that's on our line

By now you should have realized
How your sweetness is my weakness
Oh yeah...also your thighs
Cause you are physically into fitness

Lady I do not only wish to be a witness
I really would like to get all up in it
It's for a while you've been on the hit list
Your smile alone can cure any sickness

You are to be my lady
Not just for forever but for a day too
So long as you're not shady
I promise that I won't let them break you

~Jeffrey Lauriston

My Girlfriend:

Do you know what it is I see
When I am spending my time with you
I see a woman sitting next to me
Who is far more than just beautiful

I prefer sugar over salt or ice
& much rather honey than Lemon Pepper spice
Doing my best while trying hard as a man
Doesn't guarantee that all will go as planned

The only one thing that I know is for certain
Is how happy I get when you draw your curtains
I love to see it when you are fully exposed
Getting to love you from your head to your toes

I'm sure you know by now that I do love you
Shouldn't be hard to tell by all the things I do
I can imagine myself spending my life with you
But only if you'd like to spend yours with me too

Let me explain to you just what it is that I see
When you are sitting right there next to me
I see the most beautiful woman in the world
Who I am very proud to have as my girl

~Jeffrey Lauriston

Total Satisfaction:

It's alright if you have fallen
Yet it's a must that you heed to your calling
You may find this to be a bit appalling
But life is not merely about balling

It's about placing things in their perspectives
It's about how you set your advance directives
You are elite so you have to be selective
You are not just anybody to be messed with

It is better to receive and to give back
And it's okay to give so to receive back
That's how a good life gets better...believe that
God is looking to see where it is your heart's at

All we can do is just strive for greatness
Keeping in mind we're along with the greatest
You don't necessarily have to be the bravest
To rest among the mages and the sages

It is quite alright if you have fallen
In my heart & mind you'll always be my darling
My love for you is more than a chain reaction
It's in each link that I find total satisfaction

~Jeffery Lauriston

Play No Games:

What another great day it is
On this planet which we call Earth
We learn how to live and to let live
Respecting others & seeing their worth

We learn to stay in our own lanes
Just so we can get to where we're going
We simply only have to learn to maintain
Being wise & prudent as we are growing

Staying focused while being determined
Is how you succeed fulfilling all dreams
At times I'll go and listen to a sermon
There's lots of esteem if on God's team

We look forward to more brighter days
God is with us so we're loved always
Life goes in cycles & we go thru phases
All we have to do is read thru the pages

It's another great day on Earth for sure
We keep lives clean & our hearts pure
I won't stand for playing games anymore
I'm dog on tired and I mean to the core

~Jeffrey Lauriston

Internal Fire:

Good will and good intentions
Will only get you so far
Sometimes...I must also make mention
...You have to prove who you are

Your heart may be in the right place
But if a person has been hurt
They may not be able to erase
The experience that drove them berserk

Some will take away your innocence
To hurl you deep in the dark
When your back is against the fence
They're surprised you still got your spark

You see this spark which I speak of
Is an internal fire from God
A fire that is found in all his people
Ever blazing cool scorching hot

Good intentions and good will
Are extremely cool to me still
You're judged by the contents of your heart
And our Lord knows exactly how you feel

~Jeffrey Lauriston

The Best:

They success is found in the pile
Mistaking a real G for a juvenile
I rather just be swimming in her Nile
Then worry bout if someone likes my style

Meanwhile
And I do mean meanwhile
Ain't gonna let em drive me crazy
Oh no no me no senile

Lets keep it plain and sim pal
Ain't trying to be your pen pal
I like your style love your ways
Because you fit the profile for days

But I am on my way now
Seen how it all had went down
I take a bow
Revealing to her...she is the best in town

They say success is in the pile
And that may prove to be true
But a pal is still a pal
Why not be a friend to me too

~Jeffrey Lauriston

Just Me & You:

Babe I promise I could be loyal
Only if you're loyal to me
But if you would rather just roam
Then I will also go to Rome

If you were to treat me right
I'll fill your life with sheer delight
I will love you throughout the night
While doing all of the things you like

I know how you really love bread
And as for me well not so much
What it is I really do love instead
Is seeing all the lives that we can touch

I would much rather make a difference
Donating some resources and my time
To those who might need more upliftment
Whose lives are not yet as blessed as mine

Babe I will promise to be loyal
But only if you are loyal too
For there will be loss of respect
If it cannot be just me and you

Jeffrey Lauriston

Bold Love:

Girl you give me the tightest hold
For that alone our love won't fold
You used to once treat me so cold
Till you realized that it was getting old

I'm not too sure why some are blind
Wanting to be cruel all the time
Leave all your problems far behind
Cause they're your problems and not mine

Okay girl I can deal with you
I'll let you do what you have to do
Making sure our lives become better
But as for me I'm to the letter

I've got three sons walking this earth
After God I am to put them first
Now if you know what life is worth
You may be prone to giving birth

Girl I wanna come visit your gate
So I can set the story straight
I'd really like that piece of pie
Laying right in between your thigh

Babe you give me the tightest hold
A love so strong so real and bold
Though half the story hasn't been told
It is to be taught and not be sold

Jeffrey Lauriston

Tying The Knot:

My empress you are likened to a Lilly flower
Beautiful shall be your name
With my love and affection I'll surely shower
...You everyday and wash away your pain

My love when push really comes to shove
You're mostly the one who I think of
Once and if we were to tie the knot
You'll be the only one & I won't need a lot

Dearest of dearest loves who I love most
Put up your glass and let us have a toast
Here is to me to you and our lovely sky
There are no more limitations between you & I

You are part of the reason my heart still beats
It's in all seasons you make me feel complete
At least we both now realize that our love is true
...You being there for me and I for you

Empress Divine Lilly flower so sweet & kind
I am elated that I can now call you mine
A woman like you is beyond hard to find
Your loving never ceases to blow my mind

~Jeffrey Lauriston

Nobody's Fool:

Darling I love you with a passion
Not just because you are so attractive
Your love will always be in fashion
My love for you my dear is massive

I tell you that it is not an illusion
So let there be no confusion
...Cuteness it is you who I am choosing
To forge a bond with carved from our fusion

Lately you've said that you love me plenty
And that you'll never leave me empty
You are the woman of the century
It's for that alone why I do love you amply

I still think about you...that I will admit
This love spell you had me under was legit
But I am really not a duck who quacks
Nor am I a gopher and that's facts

Darling though I love you with a passion
I'm not like the ones you're used to attracting
Just because I'm courteous and cool
Does not mean that I'm anybody's fool

~Jeffrey Lauriston

Love Yourself:

I am torn between the two
& now I'm unsure just what to do
I really do wanna be with you
But can't help that I kinda like her too

This very Hot and Sour mix
Just got even hotter and more sweet
What was broken is now fixed
What was laying down is back on Its feet

I will allow God to do his work
I am just now learning how to let go
Having you both is a real nice perk
Maybe now things can be quid pro quo

If it's not an even exchange
Than any little thing can just tip the scale
I do find it to be a bit strange
Giving a girl heaven only to give you hell

I was torn between the two
But I am no more now since there is three
I know exactly what to do
Since the third person I'm referring to is me

~Jeffrey Lauriston

One More Try:

Okay I decided to take shorty back
It really did happen just like that
I'm actually the one who placed the call
Said I wanted to press play & not pause

I understand she had to do her thing
She wanted to make sure that I was staying
I promised her that I wasn't going nowhere
What else does it take to show I care

I'm not only about the chop and screw
I like to just chill letting it do what it do
We all were created with a purpose
No one should ever be deemed worthless

If someone is treating you good & right
Why shouldn't you treat them just the same
We shouldn't neither have to fuss or fight
In order for us to be able to maintain

We will go and give it one more try
Like building endless castles in the sky
Oh me oh me oh my word oh my
I can't hardly wait to go see my cutie pie

~Jeffrey Lauriston

You're My One & Only:

The C that's in your name
Represents both Courage as does Candor
The A is because you Aim
To give the best love which one could render
The R of course as we know
Stands for Ravishing and Resilient
There's also another A
Because you're so Absolutely brilliant

The L I'm sure no doubt
Must stand for luscious light and lovely
The A that will soon come about
Is there because you're Always thinking of me
The U which will proceed
Must be because you are my Universe
The R of course is to Remind me
Why it is that I choose to place you first
The I after the R
Is because you're such an Incredible star
The S as I'm sure you've guessed
Is for being so Special...girl you're blessed
The T in the last name
Is for being Terrific True and Tamed
The O as we both know
Is because you're my One & Only dame
The N that's at the end
We will say stands for Natural Nice and Neat
I will not even try and pretend
Like you do not make my life complete

~Jeffrey Lauriston

Simple Truths:

You're still my angel
And that's never gonna change
We may be strangers
Yet you'll find my love is the same

My Sweet Desire
Is what you have always been
Blue raging fire
Burns hot for you within

You still complete me
Though you're hardly around
Time for everybody
Except for the one holding you down

If you would tell it
I don't ever do squat for you
Just being rebellious
Is what you would much rather do

I'm still a man
I can't be out there chasing you
You as my woman
Know exactly what you need to do

You're still my angel
That is a simple truth today
Yet from this angle
Seems like you just want to play

~Jeffrey Lauriston

Vanished:

You told me how much I meant
Said our time together was time well spent
So tell me where the heck you went
Girl you got me bent

Had me chasing you all around town
Being nowhere to be found
Had me looking like a clown
There was bound to be a turn around

They say what goes up
Definitely comes back down
I'm not hating on you though
You do what you do cause that's all u know

We are placed on earth to flourish & grow
What is it worth treating me like a foe
I've got all of my ducks in a row
But you would rather go toe to toe

You told me a lot of things
We even spoke about wedding rings
I never thought that it would be like this
Watching as you disappear in the mist

~Jeffrey Lauriston

What's In A Name?:

Girl I cannot do it without you
Not even if I wanted to
Okay I'm lying maybe I can
But that is not part of God's plan

I am so sorry that I left you
But you know that I had to
I won't get too deep in the tails
I will come back & blaze new trails

Girl you know that I love you most
It's a love that flows from coast to coast
I will neither brag nor will I boast
No other man could ever fill my post

You see I've been there thru thick & thin
Ever since you let this player in
It's by the hairs on my chinny chin chin
That I was finally able to secure a win

Girl I cannot do it without you
Not even if I wanted to
Even if I could it's not the same
Since you're destined to have my last name

~Jeffrey Lauriston

Always Fresh:

You gave me everything that I've been missing
Your tender touch your love with the kissing
I went from having a really boring weekend
To getting to explore and tour my new friend

I never really was one to go out fishing
I went to have some fun you came by swishing
I scored a triple play with my brand new vixen
She prepared for me dinner with all the fixings

Ooh la la oui oui she is something so terrible
But when it comes to me she is so incredible
Her tenderness and beauty can't be compared
She said she'd be my cutie because I cared

She is likened to a flower ever fresh and rare
Who lets me climb atop her tower here & there
She likes to Rumba while we Salsa everywhere
I call her Babe & she calls me her Sugar Bear

You gave unto me all that which I was missing
& you're not afraid to go slaving in the kitchen
I guess I wrote this one to say to you I love you
You're number one & will forever be my angel

~Jeffrey Lauriston

Gift From Above:

Happy birthday happy birthday
Girl I love you in the worst way
Hope the blessings keep on pouring
So that true success won't be foreign

I have loved you for a long time now
Every moment shared you'd show that you cared
The experiences are no less than wows
Though life isn't fair I promise to be there

You and I had to take a slight detour
Only so we will merge to once again converge
You're my bottom you're my top and more
You are my in between being my favorite dream

It's been a minute since we last locked eyes
For being away for so long I'd like to apologize
Who knows someday soon you may be surprised
& come to realize that I'm not like all other guys

Happy birthday happy birthday
It's only for your love that I am always thirsty
You're a gift from above & I love you so badly
Our lives have gotten better since you had me

~Jeffrey Lauriston

I Still Fall For You Every day:

Gal mi love you bad oh
Gal mi love you bad oh
Gal mi love you Girl I love you
Gal mi love you bad oh

Gal mi love you bad
Because your love is so sweet
Gal mi love you bad
Because you're cool and so neat

You're the best I've had
To make me feel so complete
Mi whan fi love you bad
& Mi gwan sweep you off your feet

Tra la la la la
Gal looks like we're in too deep
Abba Ba Jah Nye
Jah guide mi soul when mi ah sleep

Gal mi love yah bad oh
Gal mi love yah bad oh
Gal mi love yah simply
Because you're the best I ever had

~Jeffrey Lauriston

Forever My Lady:

I cannot wait to see you early in the morning
To spend some time with you late in the evening
I somehow fell for you without any warning
The night we went chilling till the break of dawn n'

My love I want to see you every weekend
And really don't mind falling for you so deeply
I am so happy to get to call you my baby
Even though at times your love drives me crazy

Whenever I am with you I like to show out
There's not much I wouldn't do for you throughout
I'd like to go a swimming in your warm ocean
Might even go to sipping on your magic potion

Baby I want to love you through the whole night
I want to be there for you and just treat you right
You're my Forever Lady you're my sheer delight
You're like a new Mercedes baby let's take flight

I cannot wait to see you up in the wee morning
My dearest I have fallen without any warning
You're my shining star who brightens up my life
You know who you are soon you will be my wife

~Jeffrey Lauriston

Dreams of Brighter Days:

Our days are sure to get brighter
Don't you worry just watch and see
All you massive flash your lighters
Set your spirits and your minds free

It is on the Most High that we rely on
It is by his grace we are all saved
He is one that we can depend on
Forever & always throughout our days

Most High I come to thank you
For everything you have done for me
You've helped make my life simple
By giving me fruit from your own tree

I love you with all of my heart
My Lord you are the greatest that I know
You've given me a brand new start
From an old life that I found hard to let go

My days has surely gotten brighter
Just from your love which I gladly receive
Lord you are the pilot and you're the driver
You are the King of Kings & Chief of Chiefs

~Jeffrey Lauriston

Fantastical:

When it comes to life in general
Everything is just fantastical
Things are bound to get better though
Hold on to what you love not letting go

Love will test your patience here and there
Love is a powerful force so please beware
Love is something that needs no explanation
It is one of the most phenomenal of sensations

I'm not too certain as to whether you can relate
Love doesn't curve but it comes at you straight
Love should of course be something innate
Something from which we shall not escape

That's one of the things that I think most of
That refreshing & inexplicable feeling of love
That's what my beauty gave unto me this night
A love accompanied by kisses from my Misses

When it comes to this beautiful life we live
We learn to accept while learning to give
It's a beauty watching as new mysteries unfold
Being very awe inspiring not bound to grow old

~Jeffrey Lauriston

Heartbeat:

It's that smile of yours
That got me when we first met
That night we went out on a tour
And knew then you were a sure bet

There's times I'll relive that memory
Because of how much joy we found
Our lives are in sync and its in harmony
Shall we remain ever safe and sound

I can hear the sweetest of melodies
Resonating from your heart within
This has gone beyond mere reveries
You bringing joy into my life once again

I am fortunate to have you in my sphere
So very blessed being invited into yours
My love it's you that I hold most dear
Its always you I find myself thinking of

It is that beautiful smile of yours
That captured me right from jump
You began to allow your love to pour
Making my heart go thump thump thump

~Jeffrey Lauriston

Resurrection:

There is a man named Jesus
Who died for all of our sins
The reason I say is ...he handled his biz
And then he rose again

I let this man named Jesus
Inside my life and in my heart
Don't care too much for the Caesars
Christ was the greatest from the start

I've been in situations that were tough
And then Jesus said enough is enough
Who's perfect...definitely not me
Yet Jesus is as perfect as could be

It is to Christ Jesus our Lord alone
That I chose to give all of the glory too
The Most High who sits upon his throne
Is ever ready to help carry us through

There is a man named Jesus
Who has turned my losses into wins
Because he loves us and to please us
Jesus Christ died for all our sins

~Jeffrey Lauriston

Perfect:

When I look in your direction
Do you know what it is I see
I see the most beautiful woman
There smiling back at me

When I hear your sweet voice
Can I tell you how I feel
I feel like you're the best choice
Something that's too good to be real

When I'm there kissing your lips
While I'm holding you up close
My heart does front and back flips
Because it is you that I love most

We may have our ups and downs
Yet during all of my ins and outs
I turn your frowns right up side down
When you begin to scream and shout

Whenever I look in your direction
I will tell you just what it is I see
I see a woman carved out of perfection
Because you are so perfect to me

~Jeffrey Lauriston

Excavation:

I love you now today
More than I ever did before
You finally gave me my way
Giving me the chance to go explore

During this prolonged excavation
I discovered things that I did not know
With real cool vibes while the vibration
Remained on the setting Nice & Slow

With your help we reached the zenyth
You and I peaked at about the same time
We spent about fifty five minutes
Grooving to the song titled Bump & Grind

Right about after an hour...
Of our dancing we came to a stop
Twas an hour of sheer power
That caused me to now love you a lot

I love you now today
More than I ever did before
By bringing the sweetest love my way
Which was not so easy to ignore

~Jeffrey Lauriston

I Want To Rock With You:

Hey Queen how do you do
I'm just touching bases
To see if me and you
Could now trade love faces

I'd chase you round world
If I had no option
You are my Diamond Girl
So it is you who I'm wantin

This love isn't temporary
It is a love that is real
Just to put it plain & simply
It is you who I do feel

Our convos are now lengthy
You are finally opening up
I do care for you plenty
Q you're my true Buttercup

Q you came to my rescue
When I was feeling alone
You pulled me from the Bayou
Placing me on a throne

I know you know I got you
Actions say more than words
And I just love the way I got you
Feeling as free as a bird

Though you're twenty something
You do in fact act real wise
Just like Orion on the hunt n'
I saw you & fell from the skies

Hey Queen how do you do
This is but a quick notation
Stating that I want to rock with you
And will soon be at your location

~Jeffrey Lauriston

Nice & Slow:

We met about two months ago
That night she upped & stole the show
She rode on me like in a rodeo
Gyrating to the music sweet beat & flow

That night I'll admit I fell for her though
Licking shots in the air like Bo Bo Bo
She sipped on the face without the scar
Cooling with me & J right by the bar

We had us a really good time that night
She would not let me out of her sight
Now things don't hardly seem the same
The kisses & hugs got locked in a frame

Same story but just a different day
Babe I really do not have anytime to play
If you love me girl you gotta let me know
Then I'll nestle in your cubbie so that I can grow

Not too sure if you're just putting on a show
I promise I will slide in real nice and slow
I'll chart & navigate a course to your front doe
Its not eenie meenie miney baby love it's Mo

Say we met about two months ago
That's the night when my girly stole the show
The reason why I keep coming back for mo
Is because I would really hate to see her go

~Jeffrey Lauriston

Smile For Me:

She pulled up right beside me
Asking me if I were new
Introduced herself as Molly
I said I am Jeff...how do you do

I'm so happy to have met you
Tell me are you from around these parts
You look real good in that red dress too
Looking just like a priceless work of art

She turned pink and began blushing
Waved her hand before sayin oh shucks
It's my arm she then went to clutching
Saying I looked liked a million bucks

We got through the blase blase
Then went out to get something to eat
She said we should hangout on Friday
I said I can't hang out until next week

Her eyes then suddenly began to water
Saying then okay why not chill today
We can be together for a few hours
That should give us plenty time to play

She then threw her arms around me
Says she would make it worth my while
I said okay then just come find me
I'll admit that I really do like your smile

We did end up getting together
She really did show me a good time
Despite the harsh & inclement weather
We did our own thing from six till nine

~Jeffrey Lauriston

Awesome Feeling:

I get a real good feeling
Whenever you draw near
It's always straight up to the ceiling
You send my heart soaring to my dear

I am beginning to feel flutters
Prickling all over my chest
I can tell you that there's no other
It is you who I love best

It's a really awesome feeling
When I get to hold you so close
Hoping my actions are revealing
How it's you who I love the most

You are not just anybody
My love you are truly a queen
With a lovely mind heart body
The most beautiful I have ever seen

I may have to call you Twinkle Twinkle
Just because you're my favorite star
From the day that I got with you
I've been living like there is no tomorrow

I tell you that its an awesome feeling
Being with someone I can truly adore
I enjoy the love that you're dealing
Being a love I've not known before

~Jeffery Lauriston

Good Relations:

Do I have to tell you that you are loved
Do not my actions say that I love you enough
I know that your life has been a little bit rough
Yet you stay so strong by remaining so tough

I appreciate how I've been treated as of late
You're not just good to me you're kind & great
You even texted wishing me a real good day
These are the things to do to make me stay

You know that I will go all out for you
By always doing the best that I can do
Someday I'm sure our lives will come out okay
All we can do is strive while we hope and pray

The title is good relations since it takes two
How could there be a me if there isn't a you
I'm sure there will be a you if I am not around
I do hope to be there so I can keep you sound

I shouldn't have to tell you that you are loved
It brings joy to my heart when it's you I think of
Be my Forever Lady for the rest of our days
And I'll make it my duty to love you in all ways

~Jeffrey Lauriston

Whatever You Want:

Girl as long as you
Keep your arms around me
Girl you'll always be my boo
You'll be the only one I see

I'll give you ...
Whatever you want
Girl we'll go beyond the sky
Whatever you need
Baby, let me treat you right

Come on let me give to you
...Whatever you want
...Whatever you need
You know that my loving boo
Is something that's guaranteed

If it were not up to you
I would have never been freed
There's not much that I wouldn't do
To meet and exceed your needs

Girl you are my sunshine
And you are also my rain
Now my favorite pastime
Is being with my new best friend

You keep me going girl
Beyond the unrelenting pain
Just keep it from snowing girl
I can't bear the coldness again

I'll keep on doing my all girl
Just to keep our loving afloat
I'll catch you if you do fall girl

Just please do not rock my boat

We're gonna keep it moving girl
To the sweet beats of our hearts
Let's continue with the grooving girl
Without tearing mine apart

Girl as long as you
Keep your arms around me
You'll forever be my boo
Being the only one I see

I'll give you...
Whatever you want
Girly since I now can call you mine
Whatever you need
Come rain sleet or snow we'll be fine

~Jeffrey Lauriston

Water Under The Bridge:

You're my lady
You're not Roger's nor Chuck's
Driving me crazy
Is not what's up

We're supposed to be a team
Helping to live out each one's dreams
I ask to paddle up your stream
But you rather be cold and mean

What is a man ever to do
When you know you got one too
I don't care if it's a dude or chick
I'm not the only one you're with

You tried to try my face last time
When you wanted me to go outside
So you could rap to this other dude
This isn't Full House but damn 'How Rude

You stay sending your girl out
Showing off her cleavage and ish
As if you are in doubt
That it's you alone I wish to be with

Though we had a little hiccup
It's now water under the bridge
But you need to warm up
Girl get your head up out that fridge

You are my lady
You're neither Roger's nor Chuck's
Don't keep doing me shady
Expecting me not to give up

~Jeffrey Lauriston

Heads & Tails:

She left me all alone
Just to go have fun on her own
She never came back home
Man she never came back home

My queen left her throne
So she could go out and roam
She wouldn't answer the phone
Acting all sexy and grown

I asked her where she was going
Her friend then said what the hell
My heart just dropped and fell
When she mentioned Heads and Tails

I acted like it was nothing
Even though I was just frontin
She's all that I be wantin
She is all that I be wantin

She left me all alone
Just to go out on her own
She just hit me on the phone
I'm bout to go see what's going on

~Jeffrey Lauriston

The Answer:

She asked if I were in need
For a discreet and private dancer
Said to her I'm not in need
I could tell she didn't like the answer

I said to her no dancing
But I would not mind to romance her
Said that her eyes were so entrancing
Told her that I was mesmerized by her

Her sour face turned sweet
Looks like I swept her off her feet
The mission was nearly complete
When she wanted to start to compete

I had to whip her with my intellect
The chess match was soon over
I had her speaking foreign dialects
When she asked me to come on over

She then saw there were no need
For her to be my private dancer
Because my love was guaranteed
To keep her safe from impending danger

I Love You

~Jeffrey Lauriston

Numbers Don't Lie:

I'm torn between the two
Or maybe torn between the three
Oh wait there is one more
Therefore I'm torn between the four

All four are really cute
And they are so sexy to me
There's one who likes her boots
Not so much so for the other three

They all want my last name
Which is reserved for but one dame
Could it be Q or is it J
Or maybe it is N or C who'll stay

I know I have to find a balance
Between me and my four girlfriends
There are two who relishes silence
And two others who are setting trends

I'm torn between the four
Now two more just walked in the door
What's not broken doesn't need a fix
Great God All Mighty I now count six

~Jeffrey Lauriston

Raise the Roof:

Glad we are seeing eye to eye now
Happy we've come to an understanding
Guess there will be a you and I now
Why you gotta be so darn demanding

Looking forward to a real good time now
Already know it's gonna be a great evening
Waiting for you to come outside now
So that I can tell you how good I'm feeling

You must have fallen down from the sky now
Because you act like no less than an angel
I'm ready...its getting close to party time now
We could shoot pool and hit balls at all angles

Seems you've taken me up to paradise now
Baby I'm loving how you got me feeling
When it comes to you don't wanna take a time out
Because of all that sweet love you keep dealing

We've come to start seeimg eye to eye now
Baby Im telling you that you are the truth
I'm happy there's gonna be a you and I now
Go ahead get dressed & lets go raise the roof

~Jeffrey Lauriston

Distant Star:

Experience it for yourself
What a kind smile can do
Can't only be out for self
Other people matter too

It doesn't matter who you are
Whether you're a planet or distant star
We all originate from source
Cardinally the same east south west north

Let peace rest in your hearts and souls
Don't allow life's stresses to take control
Never give way for your rock to roll
What you give today comes back 2 folds

Many have come and many are gone
Every second another child is being born
Let's think of ways of preserving our earth
So offspring can enjoy their place of birth

Experience it for yourself
What a kind smile can do
While being mindful of self
To add a kind word in too

~Jeffrey Lauriston

Just The Two Of Us:

She's my favorite girl
She really means the most to me
She has become my world
It's only by her love I've been set free

But I don't know this girl
She'll hardly say a word to me
A stranger up in my world
Who I will gladly serve for free

Yes it was on the first night we met
Where we had a really fun & lively time
I am not saying that I have any regrets
I just cannot read minds like I read mine

It's almost a first for me
Having to brain wrestle for stimulation
Trying so hard just so to see
If she is the right one for this Haitian

She's my favorite girl
I'm hoping I won't have to say 'she was'
Because in this here 'our world'
It's not just you or me it's the two of us

~Jeffrey Lauriston

To Be Or Not To Be: (That is the Question)

I gave unto her a fair enough warning
Told her that love is all about trust
Its about respect and communication darling
Without those three there could be no us

I told her that I had no time for games
That I can play games all by myself
Her deviant smile didn't look the same
Told her that nonsense is bad for my health

I do not press on her for any pennies
I'm always just doing the best that I can
That in itself I think should have said plenty
In regards to who I am as her man

I am so far from being a psychic
I don't know nothing about any E.S.P.
I'm doing it the way she said she likes it
And all I keep getting are woe is me

I gave my lady a fair and stern warning
Explaining to her how I expect things to be
I will check back with her early in the morning
To see whether we will or we will not be

~Jeffrey Lauriston

Love You Much:

You brought balance into my sphere
I'm neither too far nor am I too near
The murky depths from which I came
Are a hindrance no more all has changed

You brought me peace where it was lost
You stuck through it all and paid the cost
Now as our reward we both get to live out
Our wildest fantasies only dreamt about

You help soothe my Chi by keeping me calm
There earlier with me sitting under the palms
Tonight it's each other we're bound to seek out
My love there's no other I want back at my house

Smooth are your tones and great your ways
I like how we converse on the phone for days
My eyes are wide open but I need not go there
Everything is okay baby love I'm right here

It's you who brought balance into my world
Since you made me yours becoming my girl
Yours is an insatiable love so hot to the touch
It's you that I think of because I love you much

~Jeffrey Lauriston

Our Sweet Magnolia:

I just wanted to start over
When I first met you
You were ranging in your Rover
Looking real cute

I asked you to pull over
And that you did
For that day you were a chauffeur
Riding around your kids

I asked you about your world
You asked me for my name
Told you you're a sexy girl
& that you were not to blame

We went on with blah blah blah's
From an excuse me miss
To laughing up under the stars
Who knew it would be like this

Used to not want to come by
Now you can't stay away
Hoping for a You & I
Just for another day

Doing everything I like
Has gotten us real far
The fact you stay looking right
Keeps me coming back for more

I just wanted to start over
When you & I first met
You're the prettiest magnolia
I have yet to see so wet

~Jeffrey Lauriston

True Love Ever Flowing:

It seems she is the anchor
That's keeping me from sailing away
My own little private dancer
At any given moment of the day

Oh yeah she is the answer
To any doubts or questions I had
I will not cease to romance her
With every single chance that I have

True love ever flowing
Is what we're gonna call this one
Tough she is not yet showing
She may just someday give me a son

Here is to the future
Here's to my now having found someone
Who may prove to be very fruitful
Who may just bear some more little ones

It would seem that my love anchor
Has brought me to a halt just in time
I've got my own sexy private dancer
Whom I can confidently say is all mine

~Jeffrey Lauriston

Forward:

Sitting underneath the lush palm trees
While busy enjoying my day
It's a nice little zephyr a real cool breeze
That I feel beginning to blow my way

Soon I'm about to go grab some Nestle
To help cool off a little and such
Riding with my lady right next to me
Loving how she doesn't ask for much

Having no time for the trivial things
Being preoccupied with living out life
By the way this girl's hips sway & swing
I may just have to make her my wife

Ding dong King as she searches for Kong
You better rep what it is that you know
With being yourself there's nothing wrong
Just ask the wind as the cool breeze blow

Sitting & relaxing underneath palm trees
Waiting outside & just shooting the breeze
I may one day have to ask this lady please
That 4 word question while I'm on one knee

~ Jeffrey Lauriston

Love Is:

Sitting here looking at the overcast sky
Waiting for you to come out your door
Has me wondering & asking myself why
Couldn't I have me a love like yours before

Could've been there before finding my heart
Shredded in pieces from being ripped apart
Tattered and battered and shattered in ways
Making it hard to recover just broken for days

Things seem more hopeful since you're around
I'm very much grateful I'm not moping around
You gave me my ups when all I had were downs
You fill up my cup with the best love in town

Just thinking about you before you get in
Has gotten me happy...I really needed a win
Seems I've hit the jackpot by gaining your love
You're my Wi-Fi hotspot that I've dreamed of

Sitting here gazing at the overcast sky
I think to myself ooh wee oh me oh my
Waiting for sheer beauty to walk out the door
She's the kinda of lady I've been searching for

~ Jeffrey Lauriston

This Is My Story (Missing Pieces):

Broken homes broken tones broken phones
Was once a unit finding themselves all alone
Were not all the I love yous suppose to last
And not becoming a thing of the past

Went from sharing something raw new and real
To seeking justice in the form of appeals
From hearing the footsteps and laughter blare
To turning my head seeing that no one is there

You used to write me poems way back then
When we were lovers parents and best friends
This day we are neither since you now have it all
But that's alright with me I bear no malice at all

What was destined to be shall come to pass
All I can do is stay focused on my onus & task
My tasks entails whatever the Lord may ask
For he is my employer and in His glory I bask

Broken homes broken tones with broken phones
Has us wondering just what the heck is going on
I don't have time to worry for all will be well
One day this will be a great story to share & tell

~Jeffrey Lauriston

Love Is For The Birds:

My little sexy dumpling
Won't you please tell me what's going on
Standing out here all on your own
Would you like for me to take you home

I will wait on your reply
Couldn't let myself just walk on by
Without sharing with you at least six words
Hoping that it isn't true love is just for the birds

Now just in case it truly is
Then I may somehow come to sprout wings
I will make loving you my biz
Thereby making you my everything

Brown sugar mind if I were to ask you...
Why is it you're full of so much spice
I believe that I have made a breakthrough
Never knew that you could be so nice

Sweet little sexy dumpling
You always seem to make my day
You are now my favorite something
Come and take my hand so we can play

~Jeffrey Lauriston

Truth vs Facts:

Oh how great a day it will be
When mankind can learn to live in unity
No more anguish from wars and death
All is to be centered no right or left

Under the umbrella of our great blue sky
We can all come to agree and see eye to eye
There are enough resources for us all to share
Let's clean up our earth changing the atmosphere

How can we come to evolve as a race at all
If we continue to divide building up racial walls
We're being forced to fight when we should unite
Never is there a wrong way to do what is right

The best thing there to do between me and you
Is to come together as one so we can make two
Underneath our brilliant sun there's nothing new
Great king Solomon knew this as facts and truth

How great a day it will be for both you and me
When we stand hand in hand against immorality
We have to be humane seeing the beauty in all
Another world war will be humanity's downfall

~Jeffrey Lauriston

My Girl Of The Year:

When I was with you last night
I would say that it really felt right
You and I we went out for a bite
Just so I could get you what you like

When I saw that smile on your face
I knew then I was at the right place
Used to say that I wouldn't give chase
Yet you left me no choice but to chase

You tried everything to make it real hard
For me to get into your sweet heart
But last night somehow all that had changed
Seeing how your attitude rearranged

I must say I am digging the new you
There's so much for us to get in to
We can kick it right here or right there
Doesn't matter as long as you're near

Quality time spent with you last night
Felt real good my love feeling so right
I will call you my girl of the year
So long as you do not disappear

~Jeffrey Lauriston

Thank You Lord:

Lord as I get down on my knees today
I would like to thank you for this day
You've given me all that I've ever asked
I love you for being up for the task

Father God I revere you praising your name
Since my knowing you my life has changed
Things in the mundane are no longer the same
Everything has transformed in my realm & plain

All will be well and all is bright
Lord you make things okay you make them right
I would like to thank you for your guiding light
I plan to always love you with all of my might

You are always there and I know you care
Lord you give a love that cannot be compared
Even though in life things are not always fair
You are there to repair my heart when it tears

Father God as I get down on my knees and pray
I thank you for giving unto me this day
You're my all you sustain me while on my way
I ask that you guard me so not to go astray

Thank You Lord

~Jeffrey Lauriston

One Heart ♥:

This color divide is eating me up alive
We're on this planet to thrive & survive
Black white green I still care I still care
Call on me and I'll be there I'll be there

Let's appreciate what it means to have life
Let's try to create a life absent racial strife
It's a bit too late to take steps back in time
Look in to my eyes I am yours & you're mine

Put our heads together and you'll come to find
That we can share one heart one soul and mind
Open up your eyes rather than remaining blind
You'll find you can relate better if you're kind

Black white purple green blue we're a tribe
If you're to be an official accept not any bribes
Do not allow corruption to sever any ties
We share a lot in common there... you and I

The color divide was eating me up for true
I stopped by to say that I do not hate you
I operate in love and so should you
It really shouldn't matter if you're red or blue

~Jeffrey Lauriston

THE END

www.ingramcontent.com/pod-product-compliance
Lightning Source LLC
Chambersburg PA
CBHW082205220526
45470CB00010B/3051